DIRT-CHEAP
SURVIVAL RETREAT

WITHDRAWN

Dedicated to my mother, who always thought I could do anything and encouraged me to try. And to the readers of TheSurvivalistBlog.Net, without you this book would not have been possible.

DIRT-CHEAP
SURVIVAL RETREAT

One Man's Solution

M.D. Creekmore

PALADIN PRESS • BOULDER, COLORADO

Dirt-Cheap Survival Retreat:
One Man's Solution
by M.D. Creekmore

Copyright © 2011 by M.D. Creekmore

ISBN 13: 978-1-58160-747-5
Printed in the United States of America

Published by Paladin Press, a division of
Paladin Enterprises, Inc.
Gunbarrel Tech Center
7077 Winchester Circle
Boulder, Colorado 80301 USA, +1.303.443.7250

Direct inquiries and/or orders to the above address.

PALADIN, PALADIN PRESS, and the "horse head" design
are trademarks belonging to Paladin Enterprises and
registered in United States Patent and Trademark Office.

Visit our website at www.paladin-press.com

WARNING

The information presented in this manual reflects the author's individual experiences and does not take into account local laws, codes, or ordinances that may pertain to your individual country, state, county, town, or city. You are responsible for researching and following all regulations, building codes, and other ordinances. It is presented *for academic study only*.

TABLE OF CONTENTS

CHAPTER ONE

Overview

The standard survival retreat advice has always been a place in Idaho, Montana, or other scarcely populated western state. And, of course, you'll need at least 20 acres, a 2,000-square-foot log cabin with a bunker underneath, a barn, pastureland, and a stream running through the property. This isn't bad advice—but how many of us can afford such a spread without crippling debt and an outlandish mortgage?

One of the most common misconceptions among survival planners is that lenders will "forgive" their liabilities during hard times. But the truth is just the opposite: an economic collapse will not protect you from your financial obligations or end your debt. It didn't during the Great Depression, and it won't now. If you owe money, the lender will expect payment or the property back. If you become unemployed and can't make the house payments, expect to find yourself on a street corner begging for handouts while living from a cardboard box.

If you *owe* for property, you don't *own* the property. If you can't make the payments on your survival retreat, the bankers will evict you, leaving you no better off than those who failed to prepare in the first place. In this regard, owning a travel trailer on "junk land" is far better than the 20-acre retreat lost to foreclosure after job loss or economic collapse. No, it's not a perfect solution, but for many it's the

1

only way to own a debt-free home or retreat . . . and the security that comes with it.

My motivation to move to the secluded abyss was more about money and a need to live on less of it. At the time I was going through a divorce and had been permanently laid off from the company where I had worked. With legal fees mounting and unemployment benefits scheduled to end in six weeks, I had to do something to avoid homelessness.

I started thinking of living in my travel trailer full time. I already owned two acres of a remote strip mine. The land hadn't been worked since the early 1940s and was overtaken by undergrowth, rabbit, and whitetail deer. I'd bought the land a couple of years before to use as a campsite and bug-out location, never dreaming I'd be living there full time, but that's what happened.

Small pine trees, thorn bushes, and sage grass surround the property. The "soil" is mostly slate rock and red clay. The closest neighbor is about one mile to the south, with the closest town about twice that. It's completely off the grid and lacking in amenities.

Everyone thought I was crazy. "Give it a little time," they said. "You'll find another job; forget this homesteading hermit thing. It's not normal. You'll never make it—you'll freeze to death."

Admittedly, I was a little intimidated. What if they were right? What if I couldn't make it? But, then, I had no choice—it was the travel trailer or a cardboard box.

I'd been brought up on a farm, so I knew how to raise a garden, tend animals, and cut firewood. Years of hunting, trapping, and scouring the backwoods had forged me into a competent outdoorsman, so I wasn't starting from nothing. I had general skills and knowledge but was lacking in such specific areas as home power generation, waste disposal, and construction.

Before moving the trailer to my two acres, I spent hours at the local library and online boning up on the ins and outs of low-tech homesteading, with a keen interest in alternative power generation and waste disposal. Everything had to be readily available and cheap

Overview

Photos of my last year's gardening and farming efforts. The garden produced corn, tomatoes, and cabbage, among other things, and the goat and chickens supplemented my food pantry.

and simple to start and operate. I came up with a plan.

But divorce lawyers and lack of funding drove me to the homestead before I'd gotten everything ready. I had to make do with what I had until I could expand my conveniences. For the first two months, I had only a flashlight, car battery, and a 200-watt inverter for power. I lived what amounted to a sustained camping trip.

Even with my limited electrical output, I had enough power to subsist. Looking back, I realize things were pretty good despite the low wattage. I'll admit that, after living all those years in a house connected to the power grid, urinating while holding a flashlight took some getting used to.

Naturally, most people won't be interested in such a lifestyle.

Living in a travel trailer on worthless dirt with no municipal hookups isn't for everyone. It takes a particular personality type—some would say the life is suited only to recluses and cranks. I disagree.

Some people prefer a life of simplicity to a "normal" stressed existence. Others want to eliminate debt and the possibility of home-lessness after an economic collapse or personal economic downturn.

Some people may be reluctant to embrace such a stripped-down lifestyle for fear of what others will think about them. To be honest, I've never cared much what people think. As long as my life has meaning to me, why should I care what Tom, Dick, or Harriet thinks about me or how I live? If you don't like what you see, turn your head. It's that simple. You'll never be happy until you stop caring what others think. Most people are self-centered and so worried about impressing others themselves, they won't even notice you or care what you're doing or how you live.

To those who fear the hardships involved or doubt their ability to live off the grid, let me assure you: your fears are unfounded. Before making the move, I too had thoughts of ruination—yet I suffered no hardships to speak of. In fact, I'm actually content for the first time in my life.

How rich do you need to be to take a warm shower, read a good book, spend time with family, or just sleep? As long as you're healthy, warm, and fed, what more could you want or need? Most of our lives are consumed by wants, not needs. We need very little to be truly happy, after we stop caring what others think.

Whenever I go into town, I notice all the newer-model cars and trucks on the road and in the parking lots and think of all the thou-sands of dollars of debt the drivers must have. And for what? To scream "look at me" to the other drivers passing by? To impress the opposite sex? To one-up the driver of a model several years old? Is it worth it? I don't think so. At least not for me.

I don't want to trade 60 hours of my life per month to the com-pany to make a car payment and another 60 or more on a home mort-gage. I would rather spend the time God gave me on this Earth

Overview

following my dreams and ambitions. I don't think the trade-off of life energy is worth the return.

As for hardships—I have none. I have infinite peace, with nothing weighing me down and no overbearing boss breathing down my neck or cracking the whip. If I want to spend the day reading or sleeping, I can. I don't have to worry about bills being paid on time. I can loaf, hunt, tend the garden, go fishing, or do whatever gets me motivated.

In the event of an economic collapse, I'll barely notice. For me things will pretty much stay as they are now. Having a paid-for piece of dirt and a roof over your head should also be your number-one priority. Stockpiles of food and gear will do you little good after the lenders take your property and throw you out on the street.

Let's get started.

CHAPTER TWO

Junk Land

As the population continues to expand, property in premium locations will sell for premium prices, pricing most of us out of the market. Thankfully, there are millions of acres of raw, undeveloped land that many consider useless or of little value. People crave convenience. The farther away from schools, shopping centers, theaters, and other establishments of convenience, the less value that land will hold for most people. But not for you because you are looking for a remote location away from all these conveniences. You can use this to your advantage in your search for cheap land.

By definition, junk land is useless property, so expect less than perfect. What you will likely find will be remote and off the power grid, with roads rough and unattended and maybe accessible only by four-wheel-drive vehicles. If you start your search expecting to find cheap land near convenience centers and connected to the power grid, you will be disappointed. It's OK to be inconvenient and off the power grid because we can take care of those things ourselves or make improvements.

Do not expect to find cheap land with standing timber, water running through it, or other resources. Instead expect land that has been stripped or clear-cut, or that is barren desert. Expect to do a lot of work to improve the property to the point of livability. But that's

The first step in securing your dirt-cheap survival retreat is to secure your land.

what makes it cheap. Buying cheap land allows you the opportunity to pay cash and avoid debt. Take advantage of this opportunity to own a paid-for piece of land and the security that comes with it.

ACQUIRING THE LAND

My Land

I found my land by placing an ad in the local newspaper. My ad read: "Looking for land to use as campsite/weekend retreat. Must be secluded; electricity and water availability desirable but not required. One/five acres—no more than $1,000 per acre." After running the ad continuously for more than six months and looking at several properties not fitting my needs or price (you will get calls from people trying to sell you more expensive property), I found what I was looking for. As I expected, it needed a lot of work, but I loved the location, and the price was one I could afford without going to the bank.

Initially, I had no intention of living on the property full time. I planned to use it only as a campsite and weekend getaway. But as life would have it, a lack of money and a divorce precipitated my move and full-time occupancy. Now, four years later, my only regret is that I didn't move earlier.

My deed says that I own two acres, but it seems like 5,000. My land is on the surface of an abandoned strip mine, directly surrounded by scrub pine and red clay. This, in turn, is nestled by thousands of acres of hardwood forest, streams, and wild game.

My closest neighbor lives about a mile away. He moved out here after serving two tours of duty in the jungles of Southeast Asia. If it weren't for the occasional sound of gunfire coming from his place, I'd probably never know he was there.

The road leading from town to my place is nine miles of winding, tree-shaded, pothole-pocked gravel. After passing several homes and a couple of small hobby farms and crossing two small bridges, the dirt road leading up to my place appears out of what seems like thin air. I'm sure most people pass without even noticing that it's there. That's exactly what you want in a survival retreat location.

What to Do Before You Buy Any Land

The number-one recommendation of those who have been and done is to never buy sight unseen. Of course, this is sage advice for any transaction. Would you marry without first meeting your potential spouse? Buy a car without driving it first? I wouldn't, and neither should you. Before buying property from any source, go there, walk over the land, ask questions, and talk to people living in the area. Never buy sight unseen. Breaking this rule is an invitation to trouble and disappointment.

Talk to someone from the county zoning commission and the building inspector. Tell the person you want to buy the property to use as a weekend getaway and that you want to park a travel trailer on it. Ask if there are any laws or ordinances that you should be concerned with before you buy.

Check with the county tax assessor's office to be sure there are no back taxes owed on the property. You want everything free and clear with no surprises. Don't be afraid to ask questions, and remember the most honest answers will come from those who have nothing to gain from the sale of the property. While at the assessor's office, find out how much your taxes will be if you purchase the land.

Research local land records, property title records, and any other public sources of information about the property being listed to be sure it is available, and who actually owns the property. If there is no easement in place and you must cross someone else's property to get to yours, pass it by. The last thing you need is a feud with other landowners in the area. If the land is far from an improved road, gaining access could mean thousands of dollars will be needed to build a road to it. Having public road frontage is by far the best option, but this is not always possible.

You will also want to know if part of the land you're interested in purchasing is being used by others to gain access to their property. If so, you could be in for a rude awakening if they decide to sue you for access across your property, or even for a portion of your land under "adverse possession" statutes (it's been done in several states).

Research the area to see if there are any other issues you should be aware of, such as water and waste restrictions, mineral rights allocation, family cemeteries, etc. Before making an offer, ascertain what the property was previously used for. You don't want to risk your health by buying a property contaminated with hazardous materials. A property that has been used for manufacturing, storage, or disposal of waste or chemical products should be avoided. Cleanup can be costly, and the risk to your health should not be taken lightly. Most land located out in the boonies has never been used for dumping chemical waste or other hazardous products, but you never can tell. It's always best to investigate such matters before making a commitment to buy.

You also want to determine if there are any future development plans for the neighboring area that would make the property unsuitable for your survival retreat. Is there a highway project or energy plant in the future?

World Wide Web

If you've looked on eBay, you've probably noticed that there is a category specifically for vacant land, with hundreds of listings posted each day. But is it safe, or is it just a big rip-off? While I've never bought land through an eBay listing, I have talked to several people who have, and their transactions were positive.

Of course, as when buying from any source, but especially online since you might not really know from whom you are buying, make sure that you do all the research discussed previously. There is no such thing as too much research, and this goes double when buying from an Internet vendor. Visit the property and make sure it matches the posted description and photos.

Before you bid on any property listed on eBay, be sure you are actually bidding on the purchase price of the property and not just making a payment. Always read the fine print—in fact, you might want to read it twice. Also check the seller's feedback rating and read the comments left by previous buyers.

Federal Government

No doubt when you start your search for cheap land the possibility of buying from the government will cross your mind. At one time this was a viable option. Under the federal Homestead Act of 1862, residents of United States, who were at least 21 years of age and who had never taken up arms against the United States, could get up to 160 acres. The law required that homesteaders file an application and improve the land by building a structure and cultivating the land. After completing the five-year residency requirement and documenting the improvements, the homesteader paid a $15 filing fee to receive title and ownership of the land.

Unfortunately, the Homestead Act of 1862 was repealed on October 21, 1976 (the date was extended to October 21, 1986, for land in Alaska). With the abolishment of the Homesteading Act, the days of free government land officially came to an end. The Bureau of Land Management (BLM) oversees hundreds of millions of acres, but you can forget about getting any of it free or below market value. I *think* it is still possible to patent a mining claim or a mill site, although the requirements are much more onerous. For instance, there has to be located there a mineral deposit that, if not being worked, at least shows evidence of values that a "prudent man" would continue to explore; for a mill site, you don't have to locate any minerals of value on the site, but you do have to be actively engaged in the milling, dressing, or refining of ore from some other believable deposit. You can forget trying on Forest Service land, but the local BLM agency could tell you if it is still theoretically possible on BLM-administered public land.

You can find out what the federal government has to offer by contacting BLM, Washington Office, 1849 C Street NW, Room 5665, Washington, DC 20240. The website is at www.blm.gov/wo /st/en.html. You should contact the BLM state office in the state (or states) in which you are interested. The corresponding addresses are listed on the federal site.

State that you're interested in purchasing land from the federal government. Ask to be notified of any BLM auctions being held within your area of interest, with descriptions of properties for sale. Ask to be placed on the mailing list for future notification of any auction or sales in the area. Just don't get your hopes up, as most land controlled by BLM is sold to corporations for commercial use. But it doesn't hurt to try. Who knows? You could get lucky.

I suggest you get a copy of Edward Preston's excellent reference *How to Buy Land Cheap*, now in its fifth edition (available through amazon.com). In it Preston covers everything you need to know about buying cheap land from city, county, state, and federal governments. You will find sample forms and letters in there that you can copy and mail to the various government agencies from which you are interested in purchasing land. Basically, you copy the letters (or write your own corresponding versions) and mail to the supervising government agencies, and they will put you on their list to be notified of upcoming auctions and of land sells.

Other Possibilities

Some of the best opportunities for buying cheap land come from individual sellers who no longer have use for the land. Heirs, retirees, farmers, timber and mining operations, and other types of owners may have land that they no longer need and are willing to sell for a reasonable price. You never know unless you ask. "Fragment" properties held by states, counties, municipalities, or corporations are a good option to explore as well. They can sometimes go begging at an auction and be had on a negotiated sale.

After deciding where you want to live, get the word out that you're looking to buy a small amount of acreage in the area for use as a campsite. No one needs to know that you plan to live on the property full time or use it as a survival retreat. Run ads in the local paper and place notices at the local post office and area businesses. You might even consider running an ad on the local radio station or TV station. Try craigslist or other online sites.

Perhaps the most productive way of finding land is to ask. If you spot a parcel that you're interested in but don't know who owns the property, find the nearest neighbor and ask. This neighbor may own the property, or he probably will know who does.

In my area there are several small logging operations that purchase tracts of property for the timber, and after the timber has been cut they move on to the next tract. They have no further use for the property after cutting and are happy to sell. Since most of this land is in remote areas, you can often buy land at a ridiculously low price. And since it has been logged, if you replant some states will give you a tax break as a "tree farm."

As stated previously, I found my land by placing an ad in the local newspaper. After running the ad for several months, I heard from the owner of a small logging operation that had operated in the area. The voice on the other end of the phone explained that he had several hundred acres of land that had recently been clear-cut that he no longer had use for and would sell for a reasonable rate.

I explained that I only had $2,000 and could not afford the entire property. We agreed that if I paid to have the parcel I wanted surveyed, he would sell me two acres for $2,000. After paying the surveyors, filing fees, and $2,000 to the seller, I was a landowner.

Real-Estate Agents

I haven't had much luck finding cheap land through real-estate agents. Most make their income through commissions and generally aren't interested in selling lower-priced properties, but then again, what do you have to lose but a few minutes of your time?

Tell the real-estate agent that you are looking for a suitable partial of land to use as a campsite and weekend getaway. Explain that electricity, sewer, and water hookups are a plus but not necessary. Real-estate agents in my state can show and broker any property listed in the state where they are licensed, regardless of the original listing broker.

Land Contracts

On the surface, buying land through a land contract arrangement with little or nothing down sounds like a great idea. It's not. The purpose of buying cheap land is staying out of debt by paying cash, which is easy enough to do because of the quality and measure of property being discussed here.

The standard land contract allows the seller to hold the title until you make all the payments. If you are late with a payment, even one time after paying on time for the past 19 years of a 20-year contract, the seller can have you removed by court order and take back the property while keeping all your money from past payments.

Another potential land mine with the seller holding your title is that he could have a mortgage himself on the property or he could lose it through divorce or other court proceedings, in which case you could lose the property and any previous funds invested. All land contracts are best avoided, as is any kind of mortgage debt if possible.

One option, which might work if you would have a seller willing to work with you, is to buy the land incrementally. As in: "I have $2,000 and want two acres now; next year (or whenever) I want an option to buy XXX more adjoining acres for $x more cash." This is subject, of course, to local ordinances regarding subdivision, etc.

IMPROVING JUNK LAND

The obvious problem with junk land is that it is less than perfect, but this lack of perfection keeps the price low and within your budget. My property is located atop an old strip mine; the topsoil and coal were removed years before. Trying to dig into the compacted clay and slate is nearly impossible, and you can forget about digging a conventional garden—it is raised beds or nothing.

Don't expect to be near power lines. I am about a mile from the line and need to generate my own electricity. This is not as complicated as it first seems: a few solar panels, batteries, an inverter, and a small generator will get you up and running. Just don't expect unlimited power. (I will cover this in Chapter 4.)

My land has no water from the city utility. It is dry land, another reason it sold cheaply. For the first several months, I hauled water to my trailer in 5-gallon containers, but this wasn't compatible with my goal of self-sufficiency. Luckily, I've since developed a spring nearby, which now supplies all my needs.

Junk land is not a perfect solution, but it may be the only one you can afford. With work, luck, and determination, you can turn it into a homestead. Just expect to make sacrifices and do a lot of hard work before reaching that point.

CHAPTER THREE

The Trailer

Travel trailers are a lot like automobiles—they depreciate in value over time. From the moment you pull the trailer off the lot, it starts to lose value. In fact, recent research has shown that new travel trailers can depreciate as much as one-third over the first three years of ownership.

I bought my travel trailer from a local man for $3,500. By comparison, he had paid $28,000 for it 11 years earlier. Folks, that's a savings of more than $24,000. Buying new is a fool's game and best avoided. Fortunately, finding a good used travel trailer isn't difficult if you know where to look.

THE SEARCH IS ON

It is amazing what you can find by driving the backroads. Many people who have travel trailers for sale will park them beside the road in front of their houses and tape a for-sale sign in the window. In fact, I spotted two trailers with for-sale signs attached yesterday on my way to the hardware store.

Keep in mind that these people are typically motivated sellers and will usually take less than they initially ask, sometimes a lot less. It doesn't hurt to make an offer. Who knows? You could get lucky.

Simply let the seller know that you're interested but your budget doesn't quite cover the asking price.

I often see used travel trailers listed in the classified section of the local newspaper or community shopper. Again these are motivated sellers, who will usually sell far below their original asking price. Sometimes it is amazing at the price reduction you can get by making an insanely low offer.

Sometimes travel trailers are listed on such Internet sites as eBay and craigslist. Over the years, I've seen some nice ones listed for $2,000 to $3,000, but most are newer models that are out of your price range. As with buying properties online, never buy a travel trailer or RV sight unseen.

DON'T GET RIPPED OFF

Be sure everything in the trailer works properly before buying. The last thing you need is to expend all your resources on the land and the trailer only to find out later that your electrical system, plumbing, refrigerator, cook stove, hot-water heater, or furnace doesn't work.

While some sellers are inherently honest and will tell you about known problems, needed repairs, or other surprises, many are not and have no compunction about ripping you off. The only way to be certain you are getting what you are paying for is to do your own inspection and tests of the essential components.

Start with the 12-volt lights. Simply flipping on the switch can check these devices. If the seller tells you the lights don't work because the batteries are dead—charge them up. If the trailer doesn't have any batteries at all in the battery compartment, use the one from your truck.

Next check the cook stove, furnace, water heater, and refrigerator to make sure everything works off propane. If the trailer's propane tanks are empty, you could take one of the tanks to a propane distributer to have it filled, but preferably you have brought your own full tank to use if needed. Whatever you do, don't buy without doing your due diligence.

The seller could have used the propane on his last camping trip, but then again he could be trying to hide the fact that some or all the propane appliances don't work. Don't forget to check the propane lines and appliances for leaks. You can do this with a spray bottle filled with water and soap. Spray the lines and look for air bubbles to form, indicating leaks.

After you are satisfied that all the propane appliances work, it is time to check the plumbing and water systems. Fill the holding tank and check for leaks. Turn on the 12-volt water pump to pressurize the system and check the sinks, shower, and toilet.

Don't forget to check for leaks in the water lines, as well as under the sinks, pump, and tanks. Some of the lines can be in difficult- or impossible-to-reach places, such as behind walls, under floors, and inside cabinets, but check the best you can.

While you are checking for leaks, feel the floor and areas around and under the sinks, holding tank, shower, toilet, and water heater for soft spots and rot. Also, inspect the areas around windowsills and doors. Look for dark spots on the ceiling indicating leaks. Be sure to double-check around rooftop air-conditioning units.

Once you are satisfied with the interior, it's time to look underneath the trailer. Check for rot, especially where the walls and floor meet the underneath area. Problems here can often be fixed by replacing rotted wood, but if prevalent throughout, I would pass on this trailer.

Inspect the condition of the insulation and weather barrier, but don't be overly concerned if it is not perfect, as most of this can be easily fixed by adding more insulation and covering with 6-mil plastic sheeting stapled underneath.

SIZE MATTERS

My trailer is 26 feet from hitch to bumper, and I still feel cramped at times. Contrary to what you may have been told, size matters. You'll obviously be spending a lot of time between those four walls, so the bigger the trailer the better. Just be sure you have a way to tow it to the site. Personally, I would not consider a trailer less than 21 feet in length.

SETUP

Now that you have your land and trailer, it's time to set up the dirt-cheap survival retreat. Trust me, this is the fun part. The first thing to consider is location. Often the prettiest site isn't the best. Try to find a spot that is level and protected from wind and flooding but that has full southern exposure to the sun and easy access.

After you've decided on location, lay two patio blocks end to end in front of each tire and pull the trailer up so the tires rest directly on

A semipermanent foundation can be made with concrete blocks stacked to the needed height.

top of the blocks. Make sure these are level. You could use wood planks or some other barrier, but I think patio blocks are best.

Most trailers come with stands underneath so that it is easy to adjust and level the trailer. If yours does not have stands or they no longer work, you can use concrete blocks instead. If you use wood, be sure to protect the pieces from rot by placing patio blocks underneath, between the wood and ground.

Make sure the trailer is level before proceeding further. This is important for proper operation of the propane refrigerator, as well as for your comfort. I used a spirit level (bubble level) across the floor of the trailer and a smaller level inside the refrigerator. When you are satisfied that everything is plumb, tighten down the jacks stands or set the trailer on a foundation of concrete blocks.

At this point, I used tie-downs to protect against wind. I drove metal fence posts, four to each side, underneath the trailer at an angle to the inside, leaving about 6 inches protruding from ground level. I then drilled 3/8-inch holes through each post about 3 inches from the top.

Next I drilled 3/8-inch holes through the metal frame of the trailer in corresponding locations with the tie-downs. Then I used airplane cable to connect the two.

SKIRTING

Travel trailers are cold in winter. Skirting helps to keep the floor warm and holding tanks and plumbing from freezing. If you are in a windy area, skirting will also help keep the trailer from swaying in the wind and allows for secure storage underneath.

You should be able to skirt your trailer in a day or two, and I highly recommend that you do it. I used half-inch plywood held in place with wood screws and 2x4 framing, but you can use other materials. Some handymen have used fiberglass panels, wood planks, and barn metal with good results.

The first step is to take off the wheel well covers (if possible) and dig a trench about 4 to 6 inches deep around the length of the trailer,

The 2x4 framing underneath the trailer supports the skirting.

directly in line with the trailer body and sidewalls. Next build a frame from 2x4s underneath to which you secure the skirting. I bolted this directly to the metal frame for stability.

Next, measure the distance from the bottom of the trailer to the bottom of the trench, and then mark and cut each piece of plywood to fit as you go, screwing to the 2x4 framing and back-filling the trench from both sides as you progress around the trailer. I found it best to start from the wheel wells and work my way around. For the moderate difference in price, it'd probably be worth it to use pressure-treated lumber where it comes in contact with the soil.

Decide where you want your access panel and make a cut large enough to crawl through (or to fit any item you wish to store) underneath the trailer. When cutting the panel, be careful to avoid cutting into the 2x4 framing. Attach hinges to the cutout and use it for an access door.

The panel at the right corner of the skirting allows access to the area underneath the trailer. This area is great for storage and access for repairs when needed.

Next, fill any cracks around the wheel wells, doorstep, and edges with caulk or expanding foam insulation, and you're done. I heard about a fellow in Minnesota who stuffed bags of dry leaves under his trailer for extra insulation during the winter. He said it made a big difference. Enjoy the warmth.

LIVING IN SMALL SPACES

In the summer with the door and windows open, my trailer is as big as the world outside, but during the winter months cabin fever can set in quickly. When living in this limited space, you must use every inch of available space effectively to maintain your sanity.

Simple things like keeping everything neat, clean, and organized go a long way toward maintaining normalcy. A sink full of dirty dishes or an unmade bed looks like a huge mess in any home, but especially in such a small space. Everything should have a place and should be cleaned and put up after use.

Be creative with the space you have available. Simple things such as building a bookshelf under the kitchen table, hanging a hat rack in the closet, or utilizing plastic totes under the bed for storage can go a long way toward maximizing space.

WINTER LIVING

Travel trailers are hot in summer and cold in winter. There isn't much you can do about that, as it's the nature of the thing and something you've got to live with if you decide to live in a tin box.

Last winter, I taped clear plastic over the single-pane glass windows and reconditioned the seal around the door. Next, I replaced the lightweight "summer curtains" with heavyweight acrylic fleece to further block drafts and keep heat in and cold out.

My trailer has two ceiling vents, one in the bedroom and another in the bathroom. These are great in summer for letting the heat out. Unfortunately, during the winter months they are a huge energy loss by letting heat out and cold in, even when closed.

To eliminate this, I cut two "pillows" from a 4-inch-thick piece of foam. I cut these slightly larger than the vent spaces so they could be pushed into the space and held in place by friction. I cut two cover pieces from an emergency blanket large enough to cover the pillows on all sides and then neatly folded and taped this over the pillows, forming a reflective cover. The pillows are easily removed if needed.

Travel trailer doors are poorly insulated and have single-pane glass. As a result, they aren't very energy efficient. I taped clear plastic over the door window and secured a heavy wool blanket over the door to block out the cold and drafts.

A similar option that may fit your circumstances, budget, and lifestyle is the housecar (aka "Winnebago") approach. Although there are advantages for certain lifestyles, an "entry level" housecar priced at $3,500 may require a lot more money to make it livable and reliably portable. At the low end of this option is the converted school or transit bus, available in every imaginable configuration, dimension, and condition. For those with the skills and an interest in a sweat equity,

I made insulating pillows from 4-inch foam and covered them with material cut from an emergency blanket to cover the ceiling vents in my trailer. In the winter, these pillows trap the warm air inside and prevent the cold air from seeping in.

this may be worth considering. Because the vehicle is often offered in such poor condition, it has given the genre a bad name as ne'er-do-wells and incompetents abandon poorly wrought or uncompleted examples to become eyesores. One excellent point of contact for locating suitable vehicles and conversion parts, however, is www.sellabus.com. Local school district auctions are another good place to start as well.

One trade-off to consider is that, with a motorized housecar, you don't have to have a tow vehicle. On the other hand, unless you have a smaller satellite vehicle, you will have to take your whole house in to the grocery store or the post office, which can be a chore if you are located far off the beaten path.

CHAPTER FOUR

Solar and Generator Power Systems

When I first moved to my retreat, I generated power by using the electrical system of my truck. I'd pull the truck up next to the trailer and connect the truck battery to trailer batteries via corresponding cable connections. I charged the batteries by starting the truck and letting it run until the trailer batteries were fully charged.

This worked well, providing enough power to run my 12-volt lights, radio, portable DVD player, and other small appliances. A more cost-effective system would have been mounting the trailer batteries in the bed of the truck and connecting to the truck battery via cables so they would be charged automatically whenever the truck was driven.

Some of you may be able to harness the wind to power your retreat. Lately, I've noticed small 400-watt wind generators selling for under $500 on Amazon.com. While I have no firsthand experience with these generators, the reports I've gotten from those who have are positive.

No doubt, many of you will want a solar-power system. There is something about harnessing the power of the sun to power your retreat that is addictive. Solar power is clean, quiet, and efficient. I've been living with solar for more than four years now, and I can't imagine living any other way.

MY POWER SETUP

My power system is small, consisting of four 15-watt solar panels for a total of 60 watts, two deep-cycle batteries, a 400-watt inverter with two 110-volt outlets, a charge controller, a power monitor, and a 1,000-watt generator. The entire system cost under $750. My power needs are very basic, and my setup reflects this.

Currently, I'm upgrading to a 246-watt solar system, which should give much better performance and require less reliance on a generator for my power needs. My advice is to get the best system that you can afford, whether that is a 60- or a 500-watt setup. When starting with a solar system, plan and buy modular components that are part of an expandable system.

Before we go further, let's take a closer look at the components that make up my dirt-cheap power setup and how they work. I'll try not to get too scientific about all this because you don't have to know that stuff. But you do need to know the basics and the parts that make up the system.

Solar Panels

Solar panels work by collecting the sun's rays and converting it to direct current (DC) energy, whereas a typical grid-powered home works on alternating current (AC). DC power can be used to run just about anything AC power can, and it can be converted into AC power. It may sound complicated, but it's not. Don't be intimidated.

In most cases, the higher the wattage of a solar panel, the more expensive those panels will be. So you may want to start out small and expand your system as finances allow. However, it should be noted that the cost of solar panels has dropped significantly over the past several years, so cost isn't the handicap it once was. My advice is to get the best panels with the highest output you can afford.

Basically, there are three types of solar panels: monocrystalline, polycrystalline, and amorphous. Amorphous panels are the least efficient, polycrystalline are the most common type of panel on the mar-

Four 15-watt solar panels bought through Amazon.com for under $300.

ket today, and monocrystalline are the most efficient and work better under conditions of low light, but they can be slightly more expensive than the other two (though in most cases the difference in price is negligible).

Either monocrystalline or polycrystalline panels will power your survival retreat, but my first choice would be monocrystalline panels because of their slightly more efficient power production and longer life.

To get the most efficiency from your panels, they should be positioned to face direct sunlight for as long as possible each day. If you can move the panels along the path of the sun, that is even better. However, this can be time consuming and isn't always practical. Mounting in a permanent location is probably the best alternative for most situations.

According to LaMar Alexander in his book *Simple Solar Homesteading,* it's easy to determine the best placement for the panels by observing where the sun is at noon and aiming the center of the panels directly at that point.

It's often overlooked, but since I'm more safety conscious than most, I suggest you ground the panels to the earth. Drive a 5-foot or longer grounding rod (check with your local hardware store) into the ground near the panels. Next, attach heavy copper wire from the negative side of your panels to the grounding rod.

Deep-Cycle Batteries

If you can't afford solar panels or your stay is not long term, standard 12-volt car batteries will work, as long as you remember that car batteries aren't meant to be continuously drained and recharged. Deep-cycle batteries, on the other hand, are made to handle repeated discharge (as much as 80 percent) and recharging over long periods, which is what you need when running appliances.

There are basically three types of deep-cycle batteries to consider: flooded (wet), gelled, and absorbed glass mat (AGM). My advice is to start with two deep-cycle flooded-cell (with removable caps) batteries. Avoid the so-called maintenance-free flooded batteries (without caps) because they are more expensive and have a shorter lifespan than the standard flooded-cell type.

CAUTION: Batteries emit potentially explosive hydrogen gas when charging and should be located away from any possible ignition source. Your best bet is probably to use the existing battery compartment of your trailer. I have mine outside the trailer resting on a board across the trailer hitch.

The battery compartment should be vented to allow gases to escape. Never place batteries inside a sealed box or container. Mine are in plastic battery boxes, bought at Walmart for $9.95 each. These help to keep the elements out and extend the life and efficiency of the batteries. In some climates, you will have to protect the batteries from freezing.

I always wear gloves and safety glasses when working with batteries. Batteries contain sulfuric acid electrolyte, which is a corrosive liquid, and you don't want this getting on you and especially not in your eyes. Also you should avoid smoking or sparks when near your battery bank. A little Windex bottle of baking soda solution may well save your eyes; a battery that is fully charged and is cross-wired can

My batteries mounted on the trailer-hitch inside plastic battery boxes.

explode in seconds from the massive generation of hydrogen. Eye protection and a soda bottle when working on your battery pack might save you, especially since you're going to be far from help.

Using more than one battery will increase your storage capacity but will require you to connect the batteries in parallel (12-volt). Parallel hookup is done by connecting the battery terminals by heavy wire or metal strips negative to negative and positive to positive. When connecting batteries in parallel, make sure that both are of the same type and age because an older battery may not fully charge or may become over-charged, and both batteries can become damaged if not matched properly.

Inverters

Inverters make 110-volt AC from your 12-volt battery bank, allowing the use of AC-powered appliances and accessories while off-grid. The inverter you choose will depend on what you intend to power but is also limited by the size of your battery bank and the output of your solar panels.

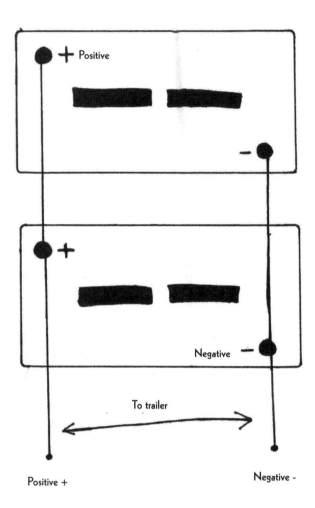

Batteries Connected in Parallel

To help you determine the type of inverter you will need, take a look at the power usage chart. The number of watts listed for each appliance is an estimate and not exact for every brand and make of appliance on the market, but it should give you an idea of what you will need.

Appliance	Wattage (approx.)
13-inch color TV	50–75
Coffeemaker	800–1,200
Stereo	50
Table fan	1–25
Laptop	20–50
Microwave	650–1,000
CB radio	5
Electric blanket	150

I suggest at least a 400-watt inverter; anything less and you will be very limited as to what you can do. Mine is made by Vector, but most brands work just as well. I paid $49 for mine and have been using it for two years, and it is still going. My only complaint is the cooling fan is a bit loud. But this isn't a big deal, since I mounted it inside the shelf, below the trailer's 12-volt plug outlet. NOTE: A 400-watt inverter isn't going to run a coffeepot or microwave, but 12-volt one-cup coffeemakers are available at most RV stores.

My Vector 400-watt inverter mounted inside a cabinet.

Charge Controller

The charge controller is installed between the solar panel array and the batteries. Its job is to regulate the voltage and current coming from the solar panels to the batteries, preventing the batteries from being overcharged and preventing backflow of current to the solar panel array. If you connect the panels directly to the batteries, you severely reduce battery life and efficiency.

Charge controls come in all shapes, sizes, and prices, and have various features. Be sure to get one compatible with the output of your solar system. I used the controller that came with my solar kit. It's a 7-amp controller rated for up to 100 watts. It features a charging light to let you know when your batteries are charging and a green light to let you know when you have a fully charged battery bank.

Power Monitor

A power monitor isn't necessary with the type of charge controller I have, since my charge controller also serves as a power monitor, letting me know when my batteries are charging and when they have reached a full charge. But the extra protection and information provided by the power monitor would act as insurance should something go wrong with the charge controller.

Generator

While a generator isn't required, it is a valuable addition to a small solar power setup. The generator can be used to operate power tools, microwave, washing machine, vacuum, and other high-energy tools and appliances. Be sure to get a generator with a 12-volt battery-charging outlet.

I have mine set up to feed additional power back into the battery bank any time the generator is running. When I'm running the microwave, power tools, or other devices, extra power is diverted from the generator to my battery bank, thus charging the batteries.

The generator works great for keeping the power flowing during extended periods of bad weather or cloud cover, when solar isn't suf-

Charge control mounted near my batteries.

My 1,000-watt, two-cycle generator is small and easily moved when needed.

ficient. Trust me, having a generator makes things much easier. Don't stint here.

My generator is a 1,000-watt, two-cycle unit made by All Power America, which I bought for $139. Though I've had good luck with mine, many people have reported having problems with this particular generator, so it might be wise to look for a different model or manufacturer. I'm looking to upgrade to one with an electric start.

No doubt some of you are thinking that you'll just skip the solar setup and batteries altogether and use the generator for all your power needs. While this will work short-term, it isn't very practical for an extended period.

A better solution (if you must omit solar altogether) would be to add two or more extra batteries and use the generator to charge them while you do other things requiring its use. And let's not forget that generators are loud and should be used with caution, or not at all, during a disaster, because doing so could draw unwanted attention to your location.

One valuable piece of equipment is a good air compressor. Adequate ones are available for not that much in 120-volt (like a little paint-sprayer model), or in 12-volt (as is often used to charge the water systems of an RV). They can be real handy for keeping up the air in all your wheels, which is important when your house is on wheels.

PUTTING IT TOGETHER

The great thing about travel trailers for quick off-grid retreats is the self-contained power system. It comes wired for 12-volt DC; all you have to do is tie your solar panels, charge controller, and batteries into the trailer's existing 12-volt system.

Mount the solar panels facing the sun, set the batteries in the battery compartment, and connect the cables. Then, connect the charge controller, power monitor, and panels to the batteries. Next mount the inverter near the trailer's 12-volt DC cigarette lighter/accessory outlet and plug in the inverter.

If your trailer doesn't have a 12-volt DC cigarette lighter/ accessory outlet (I've never seen one that didn't), another alternative

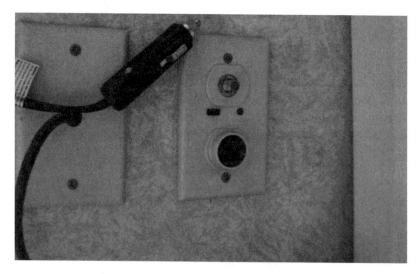

A built-in 12-volt DC cigarette lighter/accessory outlet can be used to plug in an inverter or 12-volt accessories.

is to wire the inverter directly into the trailer's 12-volt electrical system. You can also connect it to the batteries via cables leading from the battery bank to the inside.

Of course, you can locate the batteries in a different location, add more 12-volt cigarette-lighter outlets, mount the panels on the roof, or do other modifications, making the setup more complicated but possibly more tasteful and efficient.

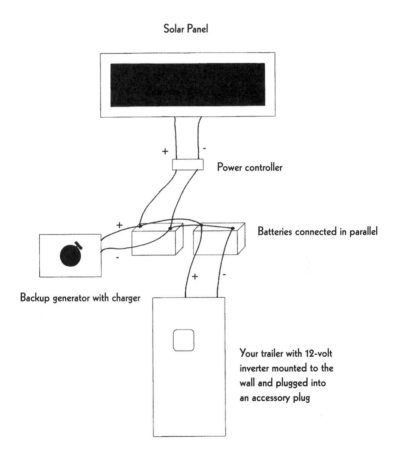

Putting your solar system components all together.

LOW-WATT LIGHTS AND APPLIANCES

To help you get the most from your small solar system, there are many low-watt appliances, lights, and accessories that will improve your quality of life off the grid.

Before I discuss ones you should consider adding, let's take a look at several that should be avoided. Just because an appliance runs off 12-volt does not make it energy efficient. For example, the 12-volt coffeepots, frying pans, heaters, and toaster ovens you see advertised in RV catalogs are real energy hogs. They work fine if used in a vehicle with the engine running or when powered by a generator but will quickly drain your batteries otherwise. The amount of power needed to run these appliances makes them impractical for most situations.

I use a number of low-watt appliances that work well. For example, the small 12-volt fans are very energy efficient. I have two, one in the living area and the other in the bedroom, and they move air through the trailer, keeping it cooler. Each fan draws about 1.5 amps. I bought mine at the local automotive parts stores.

I've also found the small automotive map lights to be useful and energy efficient. They plug directly into your 12-volt cigarette-lighter outlet. I use one to light my keyboard as I type or read at night. They also work great as night-lights.

As do most travel trailers, mine uses 1156-type auto bulbs in the overhead lights. I replaced these with more energy-efficient white LED bulbs with a bayonet base, which are rated at 4 watts. Check with your local auto parts store or do an online search for "white LED automotive bulbs." Mine are listed as part number BA15.

For entertainment, I have a 13-inch LCD flat-screen television rated at 70 watts and a 12-volt 7-inch DVD player. I plug the DVD player into the cigarette-lighter outlet of my truck when I go into town, and by the time I get back it's fully charged. I do the same with my laptop computer. This is very efficient, as I'm going into town anyway, and the power is essentially free.

HINTS, TIPS, AND POWER-SAVING SUGGESTIONS

Now that you have your solar and generator power system set up and ready to go, I thought it would be a good idea to close this chapter with a few tips I've learned during my time living off grid.

- Keep battery terminals and connections clean and corrosion free.
- Keep the batteries warm in winter by stuffing insulation around them.
- Make sure batteries are well vented.
- If possible, never let your batteries discharge below 50 percent of their capacity.
- Turn off all lights and appliances when you go outside.
- Turn off all lights and appliances when not in use.
- Better yet, unplug appliances when not in use (they can draw power even when turned off).
- Mount solar panels on a movable platform so you can move them toward the sun when needed.
- When you run the generator to run a power tool, washer, or microwave, always let it serve double duty by charging your batteries.

CHAPTER FIVE

Water, Waste, and Other Stuff

Most land in your price range will have no water from the city utility or from a natural source (e.g., a spring or stream), so you'll have to improvise. I was lucky that I found a spring near my property, but most junk land parcels won't. If your land doesn't, you will have to haul water from town, drill a water well, or put in a rainwater collection and cistern system.

I know a couple who have a huge 50,000-gallon commercial cistern system at their retreat. They use a solar-powered water pump to move the water into smaller, movable containers and into freshwater holding tanks. This works well for them, but such an elaborate system would probably be too expensive for most dirt-cheap retreaters.

A lone survivor can get by nicely in areas receiving a moderate amount of rainfall with several 55-gallon rain barrels to catch runoff. Those retreating to areas with less rainfall will need to provide for more on-site storage capacity by adding more rain barrels or other containment vessels.

Depending on several factors, several hundred gallons of water can be collected during an average rainfall. My storage buildings have a combined roof surface area of more than 600 square feet so I can collect over 250 gallons of water during a 1-inch rainstorm.

This spring near my retreat is where I get my water.

With the spring providing all the water I need, my rainwater collection and cistern system is small compared to what you may need. You will need to take a long, hard look at your location, annual rainfall totals, and personal needs before making a final decision, but suffice it to say, having too much water is better than too little.

Rainwater is best collected from a metal roof and should be filtered before drinking. I suggest the Big Berkey Water Filter system, available from Directive21.com and other online venders. (I'll go into more detail about water filters and storage solutions in Chapter 7.)

For some retreaters, drilling a water well may be an option, but this can be costly, especially if you hire a contractor to do the work. Many people have found it economical to drill their own wells using a "sandpoint drilling" technique.

While I have never done this myself, I've known several who have with good results. One homesteader drilled his well to a depth of 25 feet in two days. Another hit water at just 15 feet. They both use a 12-volt DC pump to pull water from their wells. Success depends on several factors, mainly groundwater depth and soil type.

Basically, sandpoint drilling consists of a series of steel pipes held together by threaded couplings led by a drive-point hardened-steel tip and well screen that is hand-driven down into the ground to the water table using a metal post driver (a length of weighted steel pipe with handles). Sections of pipe are added as it is driven into the ground until water is reached. This method works well down to a depth of about 50 feet in porous, sandy soils. In clay or rocky soil, it may be impossible to drive the well point deep enough to reach the water table.

If you are interested in digging a sandpoint well, I suggest you visit the Wisconsin Department of Natural Resources website and download publication PUB-DG 022 2008, *Driven (Sand-Point) Wells,* for a wealth of free information on how to do this. Well-drilling kits are available from Lehman Hardware Company (One Lehman Circle, Kidron, OH 44636) if you can't order one through your local hardware store.

As stated earlier, I get water for my retreat from a spring located near my property and from water runoff from the roof of my storage building, which is diverted into two 55-gallon plastic drums. The spring provides plenty of water for drinking, cooking, and washing. I use runoff water for washing clothes and keeping my hens, rabbits, and goats hydrated. Granted, my area gets an average of 48 inches of rainfall per year, so water isn't a problem.

If you're lucky enough to have a viable spring on or near your retreat, I suggest you download *Technical Note No. RWS. 1.M, Methods of Developing Sources of Surface Water* for free at http://www.lifewater. org/resources/rws1/rws1m.pdf, for information on developing this resource.

Positioning several kiddie pools and rolls of 16-mil plastic sheeting to divert and collect rainfall in an emergency is a good idea for every survivor, not just those living off-grid. Use the plastic sheeting to channel the water into the kiddie pools or other suitable containers. It's possible to collect several hundred gallons of water with only an inch of rainfall.

PLUMBING AND SHOWERS

The great thing about travel trailers is that they come with all the plumbing in place, including a freshwater holding tank and a 12-volt on-demand water pump. All that you need to do is make a few simple modifications to make it practical for full-time living and retreating.

Since my septic system backed up (more on that in a moment), I've used a simple gray-water recycling system. Gray water is the water that runs down the sinks and shower drain but not the toilet and can be safely used for flushing the portable toilet and watering trees, flowerbeds, or even vegetable plants if properly filtered or if you use only natural soap and no detergent.

I simply disconnected the sinks from the drain trap and placed a bucket underneath to catch the drain water from the sink. When the bucket is filled to within 3 inches of the top, I remove it from under the sink and filter by pouring through several layers of cloth.

As an extra precaution (and because it fits my personality), I use

This plastic dish pan catches drain water from the sink for use in my gray-water recycling system.

biodegradable soap for bathing, washing my hands, and cleaning dishes. You probably don't need to use this if you minimize the amount of soap used.

My shower drains into what is called a french drain (a hole dug in the ground with gravel covered with soil), through PVC pipe connected to the trailer's holding tank outlet. I used a 4-inch pipe for the drain connection. The outlet on my trailer used a 3-inch pipe, so I used a PVC adapter to connect the two together.

SANITATION AND HUMAN WASTE

Some things don't work out as planned. When I moved out here to my retreat, I spent two weeks with a pick and shovel digging a septic system, which I hoped would take care of my needs. The system was a mirror image of the one described in Brian Kelling's *Travel-Trailer Homesteading Under $5,000.*

This system consisted of two 55-gallon plastic barrels buried in the ground and connected to the trailer's holding tank by PVC pipe. The concept is simple: solids fall into the first barrel; the liquids flow into the second. Overflow is carried out and dissipated through a leach line. Simple and effective, or so I thought . . .

After I had lived at my retreat full time for more than a year, my septic backed up and overflowed. This wasn't the fault of Kelling's design but rather a complication of surrounding soil consistency. The soil in my area consists of hard clay, which doesn't drain well, so liquids put into the system failed to leach away and eventually began backing up.

After hiring a backhoe operator to dig up and remove the barrels and leach lines, I replaced the toilet inside the trailer with a portable toilet I bought at Walmart for $59.99. The same type of toilet can be found in the sporting goods section of just about any department store or online. *Caution:* You always want to do a percolation test. And there are ways of handling poor percolation in clay soil (ask the locals what works where you are).

Mine has a freshwater reservoir for flushing and a 3-gallon storage tank underneath. I have to empty the storage tank about once a week into my humanure compost pile. This is a simple and economical way to take care of human waste while eliminating the need for any type of septic system.

I replaced the standard toilet in my trailer with a portable one. This type of toilet can be found in most sporting goods or department stores.

No doubt you are asking, "What the heck is humanure and how do I compost it?" Well, basically humanure is the process of recycling human excrement through composting for agriculture or other use. If done correctly, it is a safe and sanitary method of taking care of human waste.

I suggest you head down to your nearest public library to check out *The Humanure Handbook* by Joseph Jenkins. (The book is also available online at http://humanurehandbook.com/ or from Amazon.) This book is loaded with information, tips, and advice for using this resource effectively and safely. Jenkins even includes easy-to-follow plans for building your own $25 humanure toilet.

My humanure composter consists of four standard-size tires, which I picked up free at a local used-tire dealer. I used a jigsaw to cut out the sidewall at the threads on both sides. If you don't have a jigsaw, you can use a strong knife to make the cut. It is important to get tires of the same size so they will stack on top of each other neatly as you build the compost pile.

Composting humanure isn't much different than composting

manure from any farm animal and is completely safe when done correctly. I use the finished product around fruit trees and other nonvegetable plants, but many people use it around their vegetable plants with no health issues.

After you have cut your tires, find a level spot downhill and 150 feet or more from any water or food source. Put the first tire down on the ground and line the inside with several layers of 6-mil plastic sheeting to keep the material from seeping into the ground. Next, cover the bottom with 4 to 6 inches of sawdust to absorb liquids and then dump in your toilet waste. Cover with a layer of sawdust, hay, or both.

To speed up the process, I cover the top with two layers of clear plastic sheeting held in place with rocks positioned around the outside. Solar heat increases the temperature inside, thus allowing the microorganisms to do their job more effectively and speeding up the process.

Keep adding the contents of your portable toilet as you fill it. As each tire is filled, you add another on top of that one and start over. After you've filled all four tires, cover the tires and compost with plastic sheeting. Let stand for two months. After the allotted time has passed, uncover and lift off the top tire and lay it down on the ground beside your compost pile. Shovel what was in the top tire into the empty one on the ground and repeat until all have been emptied and refilled. Recover with plastic and let stand for a year or longer. Finished compost should have a clean, earthy smell and loose, airy consistency. While your compost is aging, cut four new tires and begin a new compost pile.

Or you could also do like the old-timers did: dig an outhouse and when the hole fills up, plant a fruit tree on it.

FOOD STORAGE AND PREPARATION

Travel trailers were designed for short stays off-grid, so they come outfitted with propane appliances as factory equipment. The refrigerator in my trailer is very efficient, with fuel consumption averaging between 1.5 and 2.0 gallons of propane per week. Of

Propane cookstoves and refrigerators are very efficient and allow those of us living off-grid to retain a level of normalcy in our food preparation and consumption.

course, actual consumption will depend on several factors, such as outside temperatures and the condition of the unit.

My cookstove is a three-burner unit with an oven, as is standard with trailers this size. It doesn't have an electric or spark-based ignition and must be lit manually with a match or hand-held lighter. I've used mine to prepare everything from scrambled eggs to Thanksgiving dinner. In fall after the weather starts to cool (I live in an extremely hot and humid area), I do most of my cooking outdoors using a dutch oven or small propane grill.

HEATING AND COOLING

You could use the generator to power an air-conditioning unit for short periods, but this isn't cost-effective or practical for anything beyond the weekend camping trip. Living off-grid, you have to find other alternatives for keeping cool.

Shading the trailer from direct sunlight helps a lot, as would an extended awning. Several dirt-cheap retreaters have reported building insulated roofs over their trailers to block heat in the summer and

48

keep warmth in during the winter. Shading the trailer, whether by tree cover or a man-made structure, is probably the best method for keeping the trailer at a comfortable, or at least bearable, temperature.

If you live in an area that is not too humid, you might want to invest in a swamp cooler, or evaporative cooler. (I don't use one because of dampness and mold issues in my trailer.) A swamp cooler works fine and is way more cost effective than running a compressor-type reefer air conditioner. All an evaporative cooler runs is a fan and a dribble water pump.

Fans powered by 12-volt can be used to move air inside the trailer, but don't expect much in the way of real cooling, especially during midsummer. One day this summer the outside temperature at my retreat read 98.8 degrees; inside the trailer, with the door, windows, and vents open and two fans blowing, the temperature read 96.4.

For heat, most travel trailers come with a propane furnace and blower, but in my experience these are neither energy efficient nor cost effective.

My first winter off-grid, I heated with wood, spending more than $1,000 in five months to have firewood trucked in. I quickly realized

My heating system consists of Mr. Heater Buddy and two 100-pound propane tanks. Note the Mr. Heater fuel filter, which keeps the fuel line clean and thereby extends the life of the heater.

49

that propane would be a cheaper alternative. This past winter, I used six 100-pound tanks of propane at $65 per refill, for a total expenditure of $390—a savings of $610. Owning your own wood lot would no doubt reduce the cost differential, but, unfortunately, most of us aren't so lucky.

The heater I use is a Mr. Heater Buddy, rated at 4,000 to 9,000 BTUs. Using a 12-foot propane hose assembly and Mr. Heater Buddy fuel filter, I connect the heater directly to the 100-pound tank outside via a hole through the floor of the trailer, which I sealed with expanding foam. By keeping the heater on low (4,000 BTUs) I have been able to keep my trailer warm throughout the winter months.

At any rate, I have the wood stove and pipe held in storage for emergencies when propane may be unavailable or too expensive. I also keep a cord of cut and split firewood in reserve for this purpose as well. I also have a chain saw, an ax, a sledge, and a wedge for cutting and splitting wood for the stove.

TRASH

Trash pickup is nonexistent at my retreat, as will likely be the case in most areas off the grid. So unless you manage to find a cheap lot in town (not likely), you will have to take care of your own refuse. Luckily, this isn't difficult or costly; it just takes a bit of getting used to.

I feed kitchen scraps to the dogs or add to the compost bin. I burn paper in a metal 55-gallon drum or drop it off at the recycling center when I drop off aluminum cans. Anything I can't feed the dogs, compost, burn, or recycle, I drop off at the landfill.

CHAPTER SIX

Security

This chapter isn't meant to be a definitive study of retreat security, but rather a short overview of things you can do to protect yourself and your property while living off the grid and out of sight of the neighborhood watch.

The most common crime in my county is vandalism or property theft, but we have had a number of home invasions and several murders. Surprisingly, these crimes have happened in town. Apparently, the perpetrators know folks living outside the city limit are armed, so they look for easier prey elsewhere.

One aspect of living in a trailer that might not occur to you right away is the easy penetrability of the walls. A travel trailer offers less protection against a bullet, even a pistol bullet, than even an automobile would. For this reason I have an escape hatch in the floor under the bed that drops down into a foxhole underneath the trailer. Another advantage to this floor escape hatch is that a lot of trailers only have one door in and out, and this hatch provides an extra exit in case of fire. Plus, it gives me access to everyday goods or supplies stored under the trailer without having to go outside in the blizzard to get them.

At any rate, having warning devices and safety measures in place makes sense, especially considering the remote location of your dirt-cheap retreat.

KNOW YOUR AREA

The first precaution is to know your area. Little goes on around my place without my knowing about it. I know every tree, twig, and rock within a two-mile radius of my retreat. Frequent walks and observation breed familiarity and awareness of even the slightest disturbance to the environment.

Most thieves watch a residence for several days before breaking in. I look for footprints, broken twigs or tree branches, impressions made by someone lying down on the ground or standing, trash littered about, and other signs that someone might be casing my place.

DAKOTA ALARM

I have a motion-activated Dakota WMA-3000 "driveway alarm" set up to cover the most likely approach leading to my retreat. The transmitter operates on one 9-volt battery and is easily mounted on a tree or post to cover an approach.

The Dakota WMA-3000's transmitter uses a passive infrared beam to detect people or vehicles up to 80 feet away and then transmits a signal back to the receiver, which can be up to 600 feet away. This alerts you to anyone approaching your place, in plenty of time for you to prepare.

I have the transmitter hidden inside a hollow tree trunk to keep it out of view. I'm sure you can come up with other ways of hiding the transmitter, depending on individual circumstances. The point is to keep anyone from seeing the transmitter and possibly avoiding the infrared beam, thereby getting past this security point undetected.

FAKE SECURITY CAMERAS

Fake security cameras, which sell for as little as $20, are difficult to differentiate from the real thing. Mine operates on three AA batteries and has a built-in motion detector. It will remain still until someone passes by, and then the "camera" will move back and forth and a red light will flash.

One of these "cameras" mounted near your trailer or entrance point may scare away an intruder, and "Protected by Video Surveillance" stickers and signs may help strengthen the effect. However, I would not rely exclusively on this ruse, as most hardened criminals will be undeterred.

PAINTBALL MINES

Some have reported using paintball mines to dissuade thieves and trespassers. These are sold at many department stores or online by vendors catering to the paintball enthusiast. The mines won't "hurt" anyone, but the paint makes the would-be intruders easily identifiable (though this is only temporary as the "paint" is soap-based and washes off) and potentially scares them away.

This Chihuahua mix is an excellent alarm system.

DOGS

Dogs are great for warning you when someone is near. I have four dogs, including a pit bull terrier, but my best watchdog is a Chihuahua mix. Anything she sees, hears, or smells out of the ordinary starts her to barking and pacing in circles. I think it is more important for a dog to bark than attack an intruder, so the size of the dog doesn't matter as much as its alertness. And small dogs eat less.

Some people have reported having good luck with guinea fowl or geese as an early-warning system, but I haven't had much luck with them. They do call out with their loud, shrieking voices if concerned about intruders. But my birds are all over the place and never seem to be around when someone approaches. But both these options do taste better than dogs, if it comes to that.

OUTSIDE LIGHTING

Reliable outside lighting can be a problem off-grid, but it is necessary for security and peace of mind. I have two solar-powered motion-activated security lights, which I bought online, and so far they have worked well. The downside is that the dogs keep tripping them, although adjusting the angle of the sensor can minimize this.

HIDING YOUR VALUABLES

Hiding your valuables may be your best defense against theft. For obvious reasons, I'm not going to tell you where or how I've concealed my treasures, but suffice it to say that, if I were to die, it is unlikely anyone would ever find what I have hidden.

I know a man who constructed a hidden compartment inside his bedroom wall to hide firearms and other valuables. To anyone looking at the wall it looked perfectly normal, but he had made a removable panel from one sheet of plywood, secured in place by magnets inside the wall and metal strips glued to the back side of the paneling.

CHAPTER SEVEN

Stockpiling Water, Food, Guns, and Other Supplies

Stockpiling survival water, food, and gear can be a daunting task and is often made more complicated by misguided notions and misinformation. Contrary to what you have been led to believe, it does not take a lot of equipment or gear to secure enough food and water to stay alive.

My great-grandparents proved this during the Great Depression. From 1929 until 1937, they lived completely off the land. With the help of their three children, they provided everything for their family to survive—even thrive—during one of the most difficult times in American history.

A large garden produced the bulk of what they ate, while chickens and hogs provided eggs and meat. My great-grandfather ran a trapline consisting of fish traps set up along the creek near their farm with homemade box traps and steel traps set along the bank. When walking his trapline, he always carried a single-shot .22 rifle for dispatching trapped critters and for taking opportunistic game along the route. Every time he went into the woods, he carried a gun. He said that the family only had two guns: a single-shot .22 and a single-shot, break-open 10-gauge shotgun.

People would often come by their farm and ask if they could work for a meal or a place to sleep, and my great-grandparents never turned anyone away. They let the down-and-out people do odd jobs around the farm in exchange for a good meal and place to sleep.

My point is that my great-grandparents, and many others, survived with little more than a small parcel of land and determination. They had never heard of freeze-dried foods or MREs, nor did they have an arsenal of 25 guns, night-vision optics, body armor, and other items considered essential by some of today's survival planners.

Of course, having an adequate supply of water, food, and equipment put away before the time of need will make surviving much easier. Just don't be fooled into thinking you need to spend tens of thousands of dollars to prepare your survival stockpile.

WATER: THE ESSENTIAL RESOURCE

Having a supply of safe drinking water is crucial. Our bodies are predominantly water, and while a healthy person can survive up to a month or more without food, he can expect to survive an average of only three days without water. So having a source of clean water is a must, but how do you go about securing one?

First, you need to figure out how much water you are going to need. You might be surprised to learn that the average person in the United States uses between 80 and 100 gallons of water each day, according to the U.S. Geological Society. Much of this is used for flushing toilets, showering, and other actions that are very inefficient in terms of water usage. Just because this is how much the average person uses each day, it doesn't mean that is how much he needs to survive. How much water does each person actually *need* each day? Let's figure a minimum of 1 gallon per person per day for drinking and an additional 2 gallons for cooking, bathing, brushing teeth, doing laundry, and so on. Your bare-minimum two-week supply would consist of 42 gallons of water per person: 14 for drinking and 28 for other uses. This is the minimum amount that you should store for future use. For a couple, the minimum would be 84 gallons, and for a family of four, 168 gallons. Of course, if you live in a dry climate or an area prone to drought, you'll need to store a lot more, at least a three-month supply and more if possible.

Keep in mind, the hotter the temperatures and level of physical exertion, the more water is needed. Store as much drinking water as you have space to accommodate, especially if your stored water is your only reliable source.

Finding Storage Space

As I've said before, the downside to living in a travel trailer is lack of space. There isn't enough room for storage in general, and storing hundreds of gallons of water inside is impossible from a livability standpoint. The only alternative is to store the water outdoors.

I have my water stored in back of my unheated storage shed. At first I worried about the water freezing and bursting the containers, but that hasn't been the case, even with temperatures remaining below freezing for more than 30 straight days this past winter.

The key is to leave enough space at the top of the container (about 3 to 5 inches in a 5-gallon vessel) to allow for expansion in case of freezing. Fortunately, temperature fluctuations have little effect on the shelf life of water that has been stored properly.

An underground storage system—consisting of a food-grade 55-gallon plastic drum, PVC pipe, and 12-volt submersible pump—is probably the safest method, but it is a lot of work and expensive compared to other storage methods.

Storage Containers and Conditions

Five-gallon plastic water jugs work great for a small amount of water. These containers are easy to find at most places selling camping gear or online from most survival product vendors, and when filled are about the maximum weight that the average person can move easily.

Plastic beverage bottles can be reused for water storage, as long as they are made of heavy plastic and have tight-fitting lids. Just be sure to thoroughly clean them before filling with water because you don't want whatever was in the container to leach into the water, ruining the taste and perhaps spoiling the water.

I recommend reusing beverage bottles for very limited storage. It's difficult to gather enough for an adequate supply, and they are a pain to stack and keep organized, unless they are boxed and then they need to be the same size or the boxes will collapse under the weight.

Glass containers can also be used, but I don't recommend them. They're costly and break easily, and again it's difficult to store a sufficient amount of water in them. Plastic milk jugs are among the worst containers for long-term storage because they are unsteady, have poor lids, do not stack neatly, and are not very durable over the long haul.

Water-storage barrels are readily available from such survival product vendors as Ready Made Resources and Emergency Essentials in sizes up to 55 gallons. Just remember that a filled 55-gallon barrel weighs more than 440 pounds. If you decide to store your water in such large containers, don't forget to add a pump or siphon to make the water more accessible.

Whatever container you decide to use, make sure it is made of food-grade material and has never held any chemicals or toxic substances. Sticking with new, dedicated water containers (such as the aforementioned 5- and 6-gallon water jugs available from sporting goods or hardware stores and water barrels sold for the specific purpose of long-term water storage) eliminates this danger.

My Big Berkey water filter and extra filters.

Water Filters

I've used only a small percentage of the water filters currently on the market, so I can't recommend a wide range of brands or models. However, I have used the Big Berkey water filters (available from LPC Survival at www.goberkey.com and other Internet vendors) extensively and can give them my highest recommendation.

The Berkey filter elements are effective for removing pathogenic bacteria, cysts, and parasites, as well as for extracting chemical contaminants and impurities, such as herbicides and pesticides. The elements have an indefinite shelf life and filter more than 3,000 gallons each before needing to be replaced.

STOCKPILING SURVIVAL FOOD

The next thing you will need at your dirt-cheap survival retreat is something to eat, and any disruption in food production or distribution could leave you without. I suggest that you have at least a one-year supply on hand at all times, more if possible.

This may sound like a lot of food and it is, but it doesn't have to be expensive. For years survival marketers have preyed on the fears

 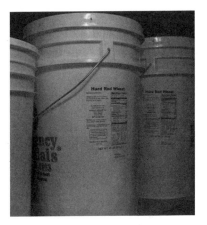

A full pantry staves off hunger.

of those waking up to the state of civilization. They would have you believe that you must spend thousands of dollars on prepackaged survival food plans in order to survive whatever catastrophe ensues.

Don't fall for it. While I have nothing against commercial survival foods, they're not the only, nor do I believe that they are the best, way to fill the larder. The bulk of my stored food consists of basic grains and beans, and yours should too. Let's take a closer look at a recommended one-year food supply for one person. Now, 500 pounds of assorted grains an beans may sound like more than enough for one person for one year, and it is more than you should need alone; the extra has been included for barter or to feed the unexpected visitor that is sure to drop by after the balloon goes up.

- 300 pounds hard-red winter wheat
- 100 pounds of legumes
- 100 pounds of other grains (e.g., whole corn, millet, oats, rice, buckwheat)
- 100 pounds of dried and canned fruits and vegetables
- 50 pounds of nonfat powdered milk
- 50 pounds of canned meats (NOTE: Freeze-dried meats provide double the serving portions of canned meats. For example, 50 pounds of freeze-dried meat would yield double the number of servings as an equal weight of canned meat would.)
- 50 pounds of sugar and/or honey
- 20 pounds of iodized salt
- 10 gallons of cooking oil (I prefer olive)
- 5 pounds each of baking powder, baking soda, pepper, and yeast
- 10 pounds of coffee
- 10 pounds of peanut butter
- Multivitamins, B-complex tablets, and 500-milligram vitamin C tablets (1- to 3-year supply)

Most of my wheat is the hard-red winter variety bought from a farmers' co-op. Don't buy seed grain, which is intended to be planted, not eaten, and is often treated with heavy-metal fungicides. I use only untreated whole grains sold as animal feed, which was meant to be eaten.

Canned fruit, vegetables, meat, and oils should be rotated, using the first-in/first-out principle. Date each can with a permanent marker or date stamp; I list the current date (storage date). as well as the manufacturer's listed use-by date on each can.

I buy powdered milk, baking powder, baking soda, and yeast from Readymade Resources or Emergency Essentials, which are prepackaged in #10 cans for long-term storage. These items are difficult to store long term without special packaging equipment, so you're better off spending the extra money and buying the specially packaged goods.

Coffee in the vacuum-packed "bricks" from the supermarket stores well; over time it does lose some flavor but is still perfectly drinkable. I store coffee in food-grade plastic buckets to protect it from vermin. Date the containers and use the first-in/first-out rotation principle.

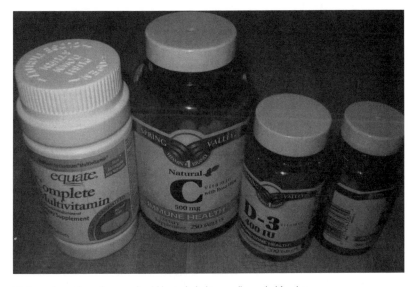

Multivitamins and supplements should be included in a well-rounded food-storage program.

Multivitamins help to ensure that you are getting everything required for optimal health. A B-complex supplement helps control stress, while vitamin C supports the immune system. Store vitamins and supplements in a cool, dark place or in the refrigerator to extend shelf life.

A supply of seasonings allows you to make even the most peculiar food palatable. I suggest basil, chili powder, cinnamon, garlic, sage, marjoram, oregano, rosemary, thyme, and others to taste. Again be sure to date, use, and rotate so you always have fresh supplies on hand. You might double up on seasonings that have medicinal value, such as garlic, tumeric, and peppers.

Don't forget hard candy, gum, drink mixes, and other "comfort foods," especially if you have children. These help reduce boredom and give a sense of normalcy during hard times. Just make sure that you and they consume a balanced diet.

Long-Term Storage

Many Internet vendors, such as Emergency Essentials, sell wheat, legumes, oats, corn, beans, and other grains prepackaged in 6-gallon, food-grade plastic buckets for long-term storage, but you can save money by doing it yourself. It's not difficult, but it does require some research.

There seems to be a lot of controversy surrounding plastic buckets for food storage, primarily what is food grade and what isn't. Unfortunately, there is a wealth of contradictory information available on the websites.

In most cases, there is no easy or sure way to tell what is food grade without contacting the manufacturer unless the buckets are marked as approved by NSF (the nonprofit, nongovernmental Food and Health Company), Food and Drug Administration (FDA), or U.S. Department of Agriculture (USDA). Buckets marked with a "2" are made of high-density polyethylene (HDPE) plastic and in most cases are food grade, but not always. If you aren't sure, contact the manufacturer to confirm whether the containers are food-grade plastic.

Sometimes you can get food-grade plastic buckets for free from local restaurants or bakeries. Check with some of your local establishments—you never know until you ask. Most of the time these buckets held icing, pickles, or similar foods, so the most difficult part is getting rid of smells left over from the original contents. Dried coffee grounds work very well and are usually available free from Starbucks and other coffee shops (tell 'em you're raising worms).

Foods stored in an oxygen-free atmosphere have a longer storage life than foods stored in an oxygenated environment. Oxygen absorbers (available from most online survival product vendors) remove the air from the enclosed container, leaving an atmosphere of 99 percent pure nitrogen in a partial vacuum, just what you need for long-term storage.

Unused oxygen-absorber packets can be stored in a small glass jar until needed.

Don't open the bag of oxygen absorbers until ready to use them because they absorb oxygen from the surrounding air and become useless rather quickly. Each bag contains a light pink capsule, which turns light blue when the bag is opened or damaged, letting you know that the contents have been compromised. Don't worry if it turns blue after you have opened the bag, as this is normal and does not mean that the absorbers are bad. This is only an indication of an unopened package, as shipped from the vendor. If the capsule is blue when the package arrives from the vendor, do not open it. Promptly send it back for an exchange or refund.

It's best to pack several buckets at once instead of one at a time. Have everything ready to go before you open the oxygen-absorber package. To fill the bucket, line the inside with a Mylar bag (available from BePrepared.com) and then slowly pour in your wheat, beans, rice, oats, or other bulk food; shake the bucket as it is being filled to settle the contents and eliminate any air gaps.

Fill the Mylar bag to within 1 inch of the top of the bucket and throw in four 500 cc or one 2,000 cc oxygen-absorber packets. If you have unused oxygen absorbers, they should be stored in a glass canning jar with lid until needed.

Next you need to seal the Mylar bag. This can be done by placing a smooth board or other suitable object across the opening of the bucket, laying the top opening of the bag across it, and ironing the bag shut with a clothes iron set at the highest setting (no steam). Many chips and snacks come in Mylar bags, which can be washed and dried and resealed in like manner. For not much, you can buy kits with hot-wire sealers for these and the vacuum-pack bags for your freezer.

Leave an unsealed 2-inch opening at one corner, tightly fold the bag into the bucket, press to displace any remaining air from the bag (or, better yet, use a straw to suck air out of the bag), and then seal the corner by crossing the other seal you just made with the iron. Next put the lid on the bucket and pound it shut by laying the board across the top and striking with a rubber mallet around the edges until sealed.

After a few hours the absorbers will create a vacuum, which will cause the lids to "pop down," indicating an airtight seal and a proper atmosphere for your long-term storage foods. Be sure to label each bucket with the date, contents, and weight, using a permanent marker. Especially if there is just one person in the household, rather than having a 5-gallon pail of beans, one of rice, one of wheat, etc., you might consider having several identical pails each with a mix of similar contents. Also consider storing lots of dry dog food. It will feed dogs and poultry—and yourself if it comes to that—and it's cheap.

This shed is part of my outdoor storage system.

At this point you may be asking where you are going to put all this food. As I have emphasized throughout this book, lack of space is the main drawback to living in a travel trailer; most supplies will have to be stored outside. I have the bulk of my storage foods in an outbuilding near my trailer.

This isn't an ideal location, but it is dry and shaded in the summer. I took a number of concrete blocks and laid a sheet of 4x8-foot plyboard on top to form a platform to set the buckets on, thus keeping them off the floor. I would love to have a root cellar or basement, but for now I must make do with this less-than-perfect solution.

GRAIN MILLS

While I can't evaluate all the makes and models of grain grinders currently available, I can tell you which ones I have owned and my thoughts on each, which should get you started in the right direction. I now own two grain mills, a Corona Landers and Back to Basics mill.

The Corona Landers is a strong mill—I've used this one for more than three years.

Corona Landers

I love my Corona Landers mill because it is strong, robust, and well made. This is the mill I use most often to grind my own grains and beans. The Corona is a hand-cranked unit, which uses rotating steel burrs to crack and grind grain, corn, beans, nuts, and seeds. It is machined from cast-iron parts; it has an electro-tinned finish to make it easy to clean and rustproof. For the price, it earns my highest recommendation.

Back to Basics

My Back to Basics mill works well and is very easy to use. My main complaint is the small hopper, which needs to be refilled after just a few cranks of the handle. It is also lightweight when compared to the Corona, and I don't think it would stand up as well to continued usage.

Country Living

While I don't own one of these mills myself, they are given the highest recommendation by those who do. A recent advertisement proclaims, "The Country Living Grain Mill is one of the highest quality grain mills ever made. You could drop it on the floor, and it would likely hurt the floor more than the grain mill. The Country Living Grain Mill is one of those high-quality items that could be passed on to the next generation." This mill is next on my shopping list.

PROPANE, GASOLINE, KEROSENE, AND DIESEL—OH MY

My fuel storage is small compared to the recommended amount by others. There is no 10,000-gallon diesel-storage tanks or resupply trucks at my place. My storage capacity is just some propane tanks and a few 5-gallon cans of fuel. Don't get me wrong—I'd love to have more, but my finances won't allow it.

When I bought my trailer, it came with two 20-pound liquefied petroleum (LP) gas (propane) tanks. These are fine for camping and recreational use but are insufficient for my needs. I quickly replaced them with 100-pound propane tanks. If used exclusively for cooking and refrigeration, these two propane tanks will last me about a year—longer if I do most of my cooking outside over an open fire or using a dutch oven. Aside from the two 100-pound propane tanks, I keep six 20-pound tanks full at all times.

Propane is efficient and easy to store in the pressurized tanks supplied by the dealer, but the tanks can be dangerous if leaks occur near an ignition source. I don't know if it's true, but the guy working for an LP dealer told me about a man who was unloading a 100-pound propane tank from his pickup truck and was blown to pieces when he touched the tank. The dealer said that the tank was laid on its side and was allowed to roll in the truck bed during transport, damaging the valve and causing a leak. When the guy grabbed the tank, static electricity from his fingers sparked an explosion, killing him and his son.

Like I said, I don't know if this actually happened or even if it could have happened as described (unless somehow an oxygen source was introduced inside the tank). It was probably just meant as a warning to me by the dealer, but it certainly made me more cautious when working with propane. Propane tanks should *never* be hauled in an enclosed vehicle or allowed to roll around during transport, and tanks should be left in the open and not tightly enclosed when in storage. I have my tanks stored outside on a platform made of concrete blocks and a sheet of plywood covered with a canvas tarp.

Gasoline is the hardest fuel to store for an extended time. I keep three 5-gallon cans full at all times. Now, 15 gallons may not sound like much, but I don't plan on joyriding through town, poking fun at those who didn't prepare, so for my needs it should last awhile.

My primary reason for storing gasoline is to keep my chain saws running. If you've ever tried cutting firewood with a crosscut saw, you know how important a chain saw is in your survival plans. I treat my gasoline with Sta-Bil (available at your local hardware store and online) and rotate it every six months.

How long gasoline will remain viable depends on several factors, such as age and purity at purchase. The blend also affects longevity; different blends are sold in winter and summer, and some have a better shelf life. According to Gold Eagle, fresh gasoline will store for 12 months when treated with Sta-Bil, and doubling the dosage will keep gasoline fresh for up to two years. But I think six months is a good cutoff period for rotation. I use the gasoline anyway, so there is no loss or waste by rotating at six-month intervals.

Kerosene and diesel are easy to store and have a longer storage life than does gasoline. I store kerosene and gasoline in different colored containers so they cannot be mixed up. Mistakenly pouring gasoline into a kerosene heater, for instance, could have dire consequences. Following a color-coding system helps eliminate this possibility. The standard fuel container color-coding system is blue for kerosene, red for gasoline, and yellow for diesel. I suggest you follow this system.

MEDICAL SUPPLIES AND TRAINING

Having a sound body and mind is paramount to survival—without both you won't survive long no matter how well prepared you are

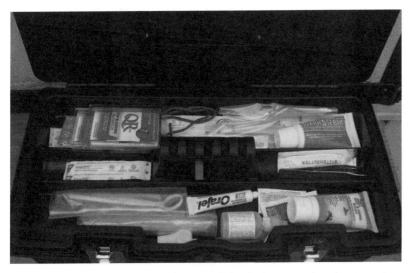

A well-stocked first-aid kit should be part of any survival plan. Just be sure you know how to use the supplies in the kit.

otherwise. My first recommendation, after getting clearance from your doctor, is to start an exercise program. Survival is hard work, and the need for physical exertion will increase as times become more difficult.

Start slowly, building up your endurance over time. You can't expect to run the New York Marathon after sitting on your butt for the past 10 years watching football, eating pizza, and drinking beer. Depending on your current level of conditioning and your doctor's orders, you may have to start out at a slow walk instead of a fast run.

Forget what that guy on the infomercial told you—you don't need the latest weight-loss gimmick or machine to tone up, lose weight, and improve your health. A routine of stretching, walking, running, and doing push-ups and sit-ups will do wonders for your conditioning. But first you have to start, and that is much harder than any exercise you will ever do.

Watch your intake of salt, sugar, and fatty cuts of meat. Whole, unprocessed foods are best and should make up the bulk of your diet. The healthiest (and most affordable and accessible) foods are those you grow and process. The old saying "You are what you eat" is critical to health and survival during the best of times, but especially so during the stress of a survival situation.

Medical Training and Education

Taking a first-aid/CPR class is the absolute minimum training every survivor should have. Nursing/home health care and paramedic/EMT classes are well worth the effort and minimal expense and will take you well beyond the knowledge level of the average first-aid class. Get as much training as possible—you can't know too much, and you can always learn something new.

There are many good medical books available to the survivalist. I recommend *Where There Is No Doctor, Where There Is No Dentist, The American Red Cross First-Aid and Safety Handbook, The Physician's Desk Reference, The Merck Manual of Diagnosis and Therapy, Ship's Medicine Chest,* and *U.S. Army Special Forces Medical Handbook* (available from Paladin Press). There are many others available, but this is a good starting point when assembling your medical library.

Home Medical Kit

A well-stocked medical kit is a must. I have what amounts to a drugstore on wheels; essentially it's a tool cart stuffed with supplies needed to treat anything from colds to severe lacerations. Assembling this kit took the better part of two years, but I think it is necessary since I intend to help others in need of care.

You can buy basic first-aid kits with alcohol pads and antiseptic wipes, latex-free adhesive bandages and gauze, medical-grade gloves, burn ointment, instant cold packs, scissors, and tweezers at most drug and department stores. You can then customize it into a more comprehensive kit tailored to your individual needs.

When expanding the basic kit, you should consider including a thermometer, CPR shield, SAM splint, blood pressure monitor, glucose monitor and test strips, adjustable crutches, bed liners, snakebite kit, antibacterial soap, Epsom salts, antidiarrhea medication, laxatives, oral and injectable antibiotics/sulfas, injectable epinephrine, injectable antihistamine, basic surgical kit, stethoscope, sterile needles and syringes, sterile IV kit, IV electrolytes, pain medications, and lots of rubbing alcohol, peroxide, iodine, betadine, and extra bandages and dressings.

Stocking Up on Prescription Medications

I consider myself lucky, in that I have no health problems and no chronic conditions that require prescription medications. But a lot of people aren't so fortunate. They need certain medications every day or risk adverse health effects or even death. Having a supply of prescription medications on hand post-collapse could mean the difference between surviving and being added to the death toll.

Getting more than a 30- or 90-day supply, at least in the United States, can be difficult if not impossible. Even if you have a sympathetic doctor you can talk into writing you an extended prescription, getting around an insurance company's "three-month limit" policy can be an insurmountable roadblock. (If you do get your doctor and insurance company to agree to multiple-month refills, there are a growing number of companies, including Walmart and Target, that offer 90-day supplies of certain generic drugs at a much reduced cost. For example, a 90-day supply of many generics can cost as little as $10, which is much less than pharmacies charge for the same drugs. Check with your doctor and pharmacist to see if your medications are eligible.)

So how do you stock up with enough prescription medications to see you though an extended emergency that could last for months or years? I know some people who have taken their prescription cards (or copies) to multiple pharmacies to get extra medications but got caught when the insurance company refused to pay for the multiple prescriptions. The only way this might work would be to pay for the extra medications entirely out of your own pocket. This could get expensive rather quickly, but if you are determined and have the cash, this could be an option. Of course, with most pharmacies being automated these days, you might not get away with it anyway. Just don't be surprised when the police slap on the handcuffs.

Some countries, including India, Egypt, Turkey, and Mexico, have a fairly relaxed attitude toward prescription drugs (this often does not apply to controlled substances, such as narcotics). For example, Mexico doesn't require prescriptions for many common medications. If you travel to these areas, picking up what you need could be as simple as asking at a local pharmacy. I have never done this myself but have heard of many people doing so. Please note that you must declare the drugs at Customs upon your return to the States. U.S. law limits you to bringing back "reasonable" amounts of medications approved for sale in this country by the Food and Drug Administration; it discourages stockpiling or purchasing large amounts of drugs for resale purposes. For drugs classified as controlled substances, a reasonable amount means up to 50 total doses.

Others have had good luck ordering nonnarcotic drugs from online sources. Just be watchful of cons and police stings. It's best to keep your dealings legal. I am by no means the last word on this, so you need to do your own research. Find out about any laws or other potential pitfalls in your state (or with your insurance provider) concerning what you are doing. Remember, a screw-up here could lead to an unwanted date with Bubba, his jar of Vaseline, and the confines of a prison cell.

The same international pharmaceutical companies that sell drugs in the United States make most of the drugs sold in other countries. However, the drugs could be counterfeit or substandard, and if they are, you have no recourse. You can't go to a government agency to get your money back or sue over damages when your source is foreign.

Another option worth looking into is obtaining medications from veterinary supply stores. Veterinary medications are less regulated, cheaper, and in most instances interchangeable between humans and animals. Dosage is usually given by weight, using pigs for the appropriate dosage, as their physiological reaction is most similar to humans.

Covering usage, treatment, and dosage in-depth is beyond the scope of this book. If you consider this something you would like to look into, I suggest you order copies of *Do-It-Yourself Medicine* and *The Survivalist's Medicine Chest* by Ragnar Benson (both are available from Paladin Press).

Preparing for Dental Emergencies

Dental problems can lead to serious health complications if untreated, but in an emergency situation, will you be able to afford competent care or even find it?

This is one instance where I think having a small gold or silver reserve is a good idea. Think of it as your emergency "insurance." After an economic collapse, the dollar may be worthless or severely devalued, but gold and silver should retain their value, which could be traded for dental (or other medical) services in an emergency.

Preventive maintenance cannot be stressed enough. Take care of your teeth. If possible, visit a dentist at least once a year (preferably twice) for to have your teeth cleaned and X-rayed as needed, and to get any problems taken care of promptly. Brush, floss, and rinse religiously, and stock up on such oral hygiene supplies as toothpaste, brushes, mouthwash, and dental floss. Stockpiling enough dental supplies to last several years can be done relatively cheaply and easily. I buy all my dental supplies from a local vendor who deals in overstocked and outdated items from a large drugstore chain at superlow prices. Even at full retail prices, the total cost should not be over $20.

Another option is to make your own toothpaste. It's easy and cheap. Mix equal parts of baking soda and salt. The result tastes like dirt, but it does a decent job of cleaning your teeth and gums. Simply moisten the toothbrush, dip it into the mixture, and brush as usual.

At any rate, it is a good idea to have a dental first-aid kit. The basic dental kit should contain:

- Temporary filling material (e.g., Temparin or Cavit)
- Tweezers
- Gauze
- Toothbrush
- Soft dental floss (an added bonus: dental floss is an excellent fiber source when you need repair string, sutures, etc.)
- Toothpaste
- Oragel or other dental pain reliever
- Ibuprofen (e.g., Advil or Motrin) to relieve pain and inflammation
- Clove oil (natural pain relief)
- Rubber gloves (some people are allergic to latex)
- Dental wax
- Toothpicks
- Cotton
- Dental mirror
- Hand sanitizer

In most all cases, it's good to have multiple smaller containers or packages, as once opened the contents of large packages may get contaminated.

You can buy a ready-made kit from many online venders, as well as from many department stores, and then expand that into a more comprehensive kit for your needs. I also suggest you get a copy of *Where There Is No Dentist*, available online from Hesperian.org.

FIREARMS FOR SELF-SUFFICIENCY AND PROTECTION

What's the perfect survival gun? That question has been asked many. many times over the years, and more than a few survivalists have attempted to answer it with their own favorites. But for the most part the effort has been in vain because the real answer is: none exists. Some firearms are indeed more versatile than others, but none is up to the task of doing everything well. There is no perfect survival gun.

You need a battery of firearms to cover defense, foraging, concealed carry, and other tasks, but you do not have to spend a lot of money. Below I have outlined five arsenals, each covering a broad range of tasks, needs, and budgets. If nothing else, my suggestions should generate discourse.

"I Work at Walmart" Arsenal

1. Mosin-Nagant Model 91/30 rifle
2. Single-shot .12 gauge
3. Smith & Wesson Model 10

"Government Welfare" Arsenal

1. Short-Magazine Lee-Enfield (SMLE)
2. Mossberg Maverick 88 12-gauge pump
3. Smith & Wesson Model 10
4. Ruger 10/22

"I Have a Full-Time Job" Arsenal

1. Ruger Mini-14 Ranch Rifle or AR-15
2. Mossberg 500 12-Gauge
3. Glock Model 19
4. Ruger 10/22

"Two Jobs and Maxed Credit Card" Arsenal

1. Ruger Mini-14 Ranch Rifle or AR-15
2. Remington 870 Express with 26-inch vent rib and riot barrel
3. Glock 19
4. Ruger 10/22
5. Remington Model 700 or Winchester Model 70 in .308 Winchester
6. Taurus CIA Model 850 .38 SPL Revolver

"Yuppie Survival" Arsenal

1. M1A or L1A1 Rifle chambered in .308 Winchester
2. Remington Model 7 bolt-action chambered in .223
3. Remington Model 700 or Winchester Model 70 in .308 Winchester
4. Remington 870 express with 26-inch vent rib and riot barrel
5. Colt 1911 A1 .45 ACP
6. Taurus CIA Model 850 .38 SPL Revolver
7. Savage Model 24F .223 Remington over 12 gauge (if you can find one used)
8. Ruger 10/22
9. Barrett 82A1 .50 BMG

It should be noted that the above are only suggestions and a representation of what I've owned and can recommend from personal experience (with the exception of the Barrett 82A1, which I have never owned). These suggestions aren't written in stone, and there are may substitutes that could be made without a loss in quality or versatility.

For example, the Taurus CIA could be replaced by a Smith & Wesson revolver of equal dimension or even a Glock 26; or you could replace the Colt 1911 A1 with one made by another company or even a Springfield Armory XD chambered for the .45 ACP.

Ammunition

After you make your survival gun selections, the next order of business is to stockpile sufficient ammunition to last the rest of your life. This may sound like a lot, but after further discussion you'll see that it isn't nearly as much as you first thought. I consider the following amounts the bare minimum:

- Big-game hunting rifles—400 rounds
- .22 LR Rimfire—8,000 rounds
- Defensive rifles—500 rounds for bolt actions or 1,000 rounds for semiautos

- Handguns—500 rounds
- Shotguns—300 rounds #6 shot, 100 rifled slugs, and 250 #4 buckshot

My recommendations are based on my experience taking three to five deer per year with 10 rounds or fewer expended. Ten rounds per year equals 400 rounds for 40 years. Ditto for .22s: 200 small-game animals taken per year for 40 years works out to 8,000 rounds. Of course, the length of one's estimated lifetime varies according to age, health, and lifestyle.

For defensive weapons, 500 to 1,000 rounds may not sound like enough, and it isn't if you rely on spray-and-pray tactics or intend to jump from one firefight to another. Hopefully, you have realized that the best way to win a battle is to avoid participating in one in the first place.

The best defense is to stay hidden and unobtrusive, avoiding confrontation if possible while retaining the goal of one-shot/one-kill if a fight cannot be avoided.

If your defensive rifle will also double as your big-game hunting rifle, I suggest you stockpile the amount of ammunition recommended for both. For example, if you've chosen the "Government Welfare Arsenal," the Enfield would serve for both hunting and defense; so you need a total of 900 rounds.

I want to emphasize that the recommendations and numbers here are minimum recommendations and should not be considered absolute. Put away as much ammunition as you can afford, but remember it is important to keep balance in your preparations.

When stored properly, ammunition has a shelf life of more than 50 years. I've personally shot rounds manufactured in the early 1920s that showed no deterioration in reliability or performance. I store my ammunition in sealed military-surplus ammo cans with moisture-absorbing desiccant packets thrown on top.

MISCELLANEOUS SUGGESTIONS

In addition to the specific food, water, medical, and weapons rec-ommendations discussed above, I recommend that you also store the following provisions for your dirt-cheap survival retreat.

- Nonhybrid seeds—at least enough for two years' planting
- $100 worth (face value) of pre-1965, 90 percent silver U.S. dimes
- A small supply of barter goods (e.g., common-caliber ammuni-tion, full-capacity magazines, liquor, and extra food)
- Pet food stored in rodent-resistant containers
- Canning jars, lids, and rings
- Feminine-hygiene and birth-control supplies (if applicable)
- Playing cards and board games (limit any games that require bat-teries or an outside power source)
- Chain saw, extra chains, two-cycle oil, spare parts, and safety gear, chain oil, chain files
- Large dutch oven
- Spare eyeglasses
- Batteries for flashlights, shortwave radio, and carbon monoxide and smoke detectors
- At least two charged fire extinguishers (an "Indian Can" back-pack hand-pump fire extinguisher is a very good investment for a site like this, as is a fire shovel or maybe a McCloud tool depending on your setting)
- Hand tools for gardening, gunsmithing, woodworking, and auto mechanics
- A sleeping bag and winter gear for each member of your group, appropriate for your region
- Box of 4-mil plastic sheeting
- Paracord, 1,000-foot roll
- $20 worth of wooden kitchen matches
- A high-quality belt knife for each member of your group

- Coleman lantern, camp stove, extra mantle, and fuel
- Wire
- Duct tape
- Small rope
- Nylon string
- Petroleum jelly
- Battery-less (hand crank or shake) flashlights and radio
- Small tentage
- Ponchos, space blankets
- Razors
- Spare kitchen tools (e.g., can opener, bottle opener)
- Food storage (Ziploc) bags
- Magnifying glass
- Epoxy adhesive
- Spare bulbs
- Candles
- Disposable butane lighters
- Toilet paper
- Booze (small bottles to trade, big bottles to use)
- Tobacco products and patent medicines to trade

When considering the recommendations given in this chapter, please understand that there is no way of knowing for certain what you'll need or how much. In the end you'll need to look at your location, needs, and budget, and plan accordingly.

Resources

- *The Encyclopedia of Country Living* by Carla Emery (covers a wealth of information)
- *The New Self-Sufficient Gardener* by John Seymour (the only gardening book you will ever need)
- *Where There Is No Doctor: A Village Health Care Handbook* and *Where There Is No Dentist* by Hesperian Foundation (medical and health care under primitive conditions)
- *Cookin' with Home Storage* by Peggy Layton and Vicki Tate (cooking and using basic storage foods)
- *How to Live without Electricity—And Like It* by Anita Evangelista (title says it all)
- *Barnyard in Your Backyard* by Gail Damerow (a beginner's guide to raising chickens, ducks, geese, rabbits, goats, sheep, and cows)
- *Putting Food By* by Janet Greene (freezing, canning, and preserving food)
- *Emergency Food Storage and Survival Handbook* by Peggy Layton (food storage and emergency preparedness)
- *Boston's Gun Bible* by Boston T. Party (firearms and gear)
- *Survival Poaching* by Ragnar Benson (wild game procurement)
- *Life after Doomsday* by Bruce Clayton (surviving a nuclear nightmare)

- *Eating Cheap* by Ragnar Benson (as the title implies)
- *Live Off the Land in the City and Country* by Ragnar Benson (as the title implies)